Dear Family,

What's the best way to help your child love reading?

Find good books like this one to share—and read together!

Here are some tips.

● **Take a "picture walk."** Look at all the pictures before you read. Talk about what you see.

● **Take turns.** Read to your child. Ham it up! Use different voices for different characters, and read with feeling! Then listen as your child reads to you, or explains the story in his or her own words.

● **Point out words as you read.** Help your child notice how letters and sounds go together. Point out unusual or difficult words that your child might not know. Talk about those words and what they mean.

● **Ask questions.** Stop to ask questions as you read. For example: "What do you think will happen next?" "How would you feel if that happened to you?"

● **Read every day.** Good stories are worth reading more than once! Read signs, labels, and even cereal boxes with your child. Visit the library to take out more books. And look for other JUST FOR YOU! BOOKS you and your child can share!

The Editors

To all of us who must find our own identity
and our own place!
—WH

For my beautiful wife Nikki,
my brothers Chris and Steve, my sister Stephanie,
and my mother.
—MP

Text copyright © 2004 by Wade Hudson.
Illustrations copyright © 2004 by Mark Page.
Produced for Scholastic by COLOR-BRIDGE BOOKS, LLC, Brooklyn, NY
All rights reserved. Published by SCHOLASTIC INC.
JUST FOR YOU! is a trademark of Scholastic Inc.

Library of Congress Cataloging-in-Publication Data

Hudson, Wade
    The two Tyrones / by Wade Hudson ; illustrated by Mark Page.
        p. cm.—(Just for You! Level 3)
    Summary: Tyrone Rashon Williams' excitement about the first day of the
new school year wanes when he sees that everyone is wearing the same new
sneakers he is so proud of, but it gets worse when a new student arrives who
has his exact same name.
    ISBN 0-439-56866-8 (pbk.)
    [1. Schools—Fiction. 2. Identity—Fiction 3. African Americans—Fiction.]
    I. Page, Mark (Mark Jason), ill. II. Title. III. Series.
    PZ7.H868Tw2004
    [E]—dc22   2004042912

10 9 8 7   09 10 11 12 13/0
    Printed in the U.S.A. 23 • First Scholastic Printing, February 2004

THE Two Tyrones

by Wade Hudson
Illustrated by Mark Page

JUST FOR YOU!™ Level 3

It was the first day of a new school year. Tyrone was excited about seeing his school friends again. More than that, Tyrone wanted to show off his new sneakers.

"Tyrone Rashon Williams! Those sneakers are not the reason you're going to school," his mother told him.

"I know, Mom."

"All right. Just don't get carried away," she said.

Tyrone had bought the sneakers with his own money. He had done errands all summer to earn enough. His sneakers were the newest brand. Tyrone just knew he'd be the first one in his class to have a pair.

When Tyrone reached the schoolyard, he saw his best friend, Jamal.

"Look! We're wearing the same sneakers," Jamal said proudly.

Tyrone looked at Jamal's feet.

Sure enough, Jamal had on the same sneakers. Same brand! Same color!

"Yeah," Tyrone said, "same sneakers." He didn't feel as excited as he had on his way to school.

When Tyrone entered the school building, almost every boy he saw had on a pair of his sneakers! His first day of school was not off to a very good start. What else could go wrong?

Soon Tyrone's class was busy working. A tall boy walked into the room. He gave the teacher a slip of paper.

Mrs. Crosby read the paper and smiled. "Class, meet Tyrone Rashon Williams," she said.

"Welcome to our school," she told the new boy. "Isn't that amazing? Now we have two Tyrone Rashon Williamses in our class!"

Jamal elbowed Tyrone. "He's got your name!" he said. "Two Tyrones. We've got two Tyrones."

"Snaps!" Tyrone said. "What a bummer!" He watched the new boy take his seat.

"He's got sneakers like mine, too!"
Tyrone sighed. He laid his head on his
desk. No, this was not a good first day
for Tyrone!

Every time Mrs. Crosby called the name Tyrone, the other Tyrone answered. Even when the teacher meant the old Tyrone, the new Tyrone would answer!

When Tyrone got home, he told his mother about his first day.

"I told you not to get carried away with those sneakers," she said. "And so what if someone else has your name?"

"But he answers when the teacher calls on me. He even answers when my **friends** call me!"

"Give it a few days, Son. Your class needs time to get used to life with two Tyrones."

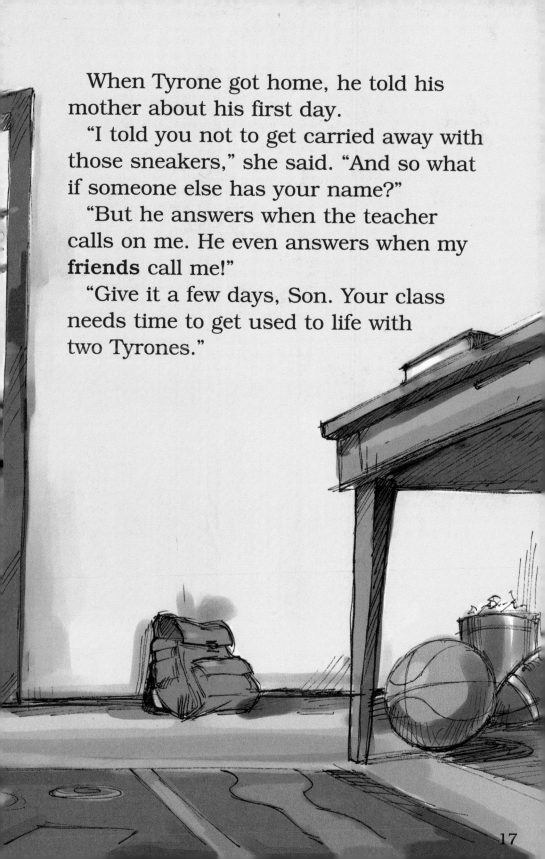

But after a few days, it was still a problem. During math, Mrs. Crosby asked, "Tyrone, will you write the answers on the board?"

Both Tyrones got up and reached for the chalk. The class exploded with laughter.

Another day, at recess, the new Tyrone threw a ball. He accidentally hit a third grader! He never even got a chance to say he was sorry.

When the principal heard about it, he sent for the old Tyrone. "What's gotten into you, Tyrone?" asked Mr. Jarvis. You've always been one of our best students."

"But it wasn't me!" cried Tyrone.

"Who was it, then?" asked the principal.

"It must have been the other Tyrone Williams—the **new** Tyrone."

"The new Tyrone?"

"Yes, Sir," answered Tyrone.

"That's right!" Suddenly Mr. Jarvis remembered. "There's a new boy whose name is Tyrone Williams, too. I'm sorry, Tyrone. Go back to your classroom. We'll straighten this all out."

Tyrone decided that he had to do
something himself. He couldn't go
through a whole school year being
mistaken for someone else! At dinner,
he shared his problem with his father.

"There has to be an answer," said Dad. "Just think about it."

Tyrone thought for a while. "I have it!" he said. "One of us can use a nickname. I could use T.R., my initials."

"Good idea," said Dad. "Why don't you ask the new Tyrone what he thinks? I'm sure he doesn't like getting mistaken for you, either."

"I'll ask him first thing tomorrow," said Tyrone. "Thanks, Dad."

His father smiled. "Don't thank me, Son. You thought of it yourself!"

The next day, the two Tyrones talked about their problem. "It's confusing for two people in the same class to have the same name," the old Tyrone said.

"I know," said the new Tyrone, "but what can we do?"

"One of us could use a nickname."

The new Tyrone thought about that. . . . "Solid!" he said. "They call me T.R. at home, and I like it. I'll tell everyone to call me T.R."

"But that's what I cho...!" the old
Tyrone started to say. Then he thought,
"If the new Tyrone calls himself T.R., I'll
be the one and only Tyrone!" So the old
Tyrone said, "Okay, I'm down with that!"

From that day on, everyone called the new Tyrone, T.R. (Except, of course, when Mrs. Crosby called the roll.)

But that was all right with the old Tyrone. He knew he'd be the one and only Tyrone for the rest of the day.

Besides, the new Tyrone—or rather T.R.—had become a good friend!

▲▲▲▲▲ JUST FOR YOU ▲▲▲▲▲

Here are some fun things for you to do.

YOUR First Day!

The **old** Tyrone had some surprises on his first day of school! Think of some things that made him feel bad. How would YOU feel if those things happened to you?

The author doesn't tell us how the **new** Tyrone felt about his first day! How do YOU think he felt?

Can you remember YOUR first day of the school year? Were you excited? Or nervous? Write a story about your first day. Draw pictures to go with it!

What's in a Nickname?

The new Tyrone decides to use the nickname T.R. Why did he pick this nickname?

A nickname can be a short form of your real name—such as "Ty" for Tyrone, or "Mike" for Michael.

A nickname can even be a description of how you look—like "Stretch" or "Red."

Pick a new nickname for yourself! What would YOU want people to call you? Why?

▲▲▲▲TOGETHER TIME ▲▲▲▲

Make some time to share ideas about the story with your young reader! Here are some activities you can try.

Talk About It: The people in this story act very much like people do in real life. Do any of the characters remind you or your child of people you know? Talk about who and why!

Think About It: The old Tyrone thought of a way to solve his problem. Point out that there is often more than one way to solve a problem! Ask your child, "Can you think of another way the two Tyrones could have dealt with their situation? What else could they have done?"

Act It Out: Ask your child to pick out his or her favorite part of the story. Then read that part together, as if it is a play or a TV script. Your child can be the old Tyrone and read all his words of dialogue. You can read the rest of the words. Remember to read with feeling!

Meet the Author

WADE HUDSON says, "My father and I have the same name. He is Wade Hudson, Sr. and I am Wade Hudson, Jr. When I was growing up, my friends would call and ask to speak with Wade. When members of my family answered, they'd ask, "Which one?" Sometimes my dad actually took calls that were meant for me. Now I appreciate how special it is to be named after my father. But when I was young, I wanted to have my own special name and identity."

Wade Hudson has written or edited more than twenty books and anthologies for young readers. He grew up in rural Mansfield, Louisiana, where he could run barefoot in the grass, pick wild berries, and play baseball. In 1988, he and his wife Cheryl started their own publishing company, Just Us Books, Inc., because they wanted young people to learn more about African Americans, their history, and their culture. Their company is located in East Orange, New Jersey, where they also live.

▲▲▲▲▲▲▲▲▲▲▲▲▲▲▲▲▲▲▲

Meet the Artist

MARK PAGE says, "When I was in school, being original was very important. If you were the only one to have a certain pair of sneakers, you earned cool points with your friends. I really felt for Tyrone when everybody showed up with the same sneakers he had! I understood why he was so upset when the new Tyrone arrived. But I especially liked the way he turned a negative into a positive!"

Mark Page graduated from the Art Center College of Design in Pasadena, California; then worked for the Walt Disney Company as a designer for several years. His first book in the JUST FOR YOU! series, *No Boys Allowed!*, was published in 2003. Mark lives in Pasadena with his wife, Nikki.